HOLY GHOST EXPLOSION

To my inspiration.
Thank you. Love

Patricia Davis

Other Books by Patricia E. Davis
_____

Thought for the Week:

Other Books by True Vine Publishing
_____

Words of My Mouth, Meditations of My Heart by:
Leah Ayanna Brown (ISBN 0-9760914-3-2)

Journeys In the Spirit by: J. Lynn Clemmons
(ISBN 0-9760914-5-3)

Dare I Ask, What Am I Afraid Of?
By: Misha A. Maynard
(ISBN 0-9760914-45)

Seasons Come by: Courtney McCoy Waller
(ISBN 0-9760914-0-2)

His Beauty for My Ashes by: S. C. Jamison
(ISBN 1-932203-79-6)

I Hear God in My Head by: Valisa R. Griffin
(ISBN 1-932203-89-3)

Charge the Walls by: Timothy O. Bond
(ISBN 1-932203-89-3)

HOLY GHOST EXPLOSION

PATRICIA E. DAVIS

TRUE VINE PUBLISHING CO.
NASHVILLE, TENN.

Holy Ghost Explosion

Published by

True Vine Publishing Co. P.O. Box 22448, Nashville, TN 37202

ISBN 0-9760914-6-1

Library of Congress Control Number: 2006900530

All scriptures, unless otherwise noted, are taken from the Holy Bible, King James Version. Used by permission.

Cover design by Elisha Vernon / kozmyq1designs

Diagrams created by Adrian J.R. Davis

Back cover photo by Emmanuel Roland/ Roland Photography

Printed in the United States of America — First printing

To place orders for book or get current information, contact us at www. truevinepublishing.com

ACKNOWLEDGMENTS

I thank God for His Spirit who has placed in me the ability to share with you gold nuggets that will assist you in releasing the power within. I thank God for my darling mother, Mrs. Dorothy G. Cheek, who taught, trained, and loved me with an everlasting love. I thank her for the time and the sharing that made her a very intricate part in my entire life.

I thank God for my husband, Thomas, who has taught me how to walk worthy of my calling and has been by my side in all of my endeavors. To my sons, Emmanuel, Adrian, and Christopher, I thank God for young men who have loved me and been there to support my every call. I thank Bishop Jerry L. Maynard who recognized the call on my life and allowed me to begin a teaching series on the Holy Ghost and gave me the opportunity to develop the gifts that God had in me.

TABLE OF CONTENTS

PART I

PART II

INTRODUCTION

The world began with the significant word "Let." God was so powerful that, in His speaking, the heavens and earth were created and all of the necessary things to bring forth abundance. God was neither a selfish God nor a God who would not share His power, so He created man in His image to have the authority over the total universe. How would this mission be accomplished?

How would the world remain in its perfect state with man in control? God, being all knowing and all powerful, knew man would fall because of his desire to be equal with Him rather than be happy about being in His image. God's plan was to allow man to learn obedience by the things that he would suffer. God's Spirit would allow man to have power over the enemy, conquer the unconquerable, soar to heights unknown, and thereby be victorious over many battles. God's grace and mercy would always be extended to man and by God's Spirit man would be reconciled to God.

In the beginning was the Word which was God and His great big universe. Because of the love for Himself,

He decided to duplicate His mighty acts of kindness, joy, peace, and grace. He decided to wrap Himself in flesh and come to the earth in the form of His Son, Jesus, whose love was so great that He left a contract with all believers concerning their past, present, and future state. Jesus Christ was so concerned about mankind that He would not leave all until His mission was completed, then He would return to put the final seal on incarnation power revealed.

Assured of the love that His Father had for humanity and the love that He knew He had for humankind, He returned to comfort and to charge the men of old that He had risen and that they must spread the word of His goodness, mercy, truth, love and saving power. The only way humanity could do this was through the power of the Holy Ghost, Christ's Spirit, Christ's power from the Father, therefore, allowing God's total plan to be revealed.

Holy Ghost Explosion is about the explosiveness of God in man and how man's fall was not an error, but was a part of the plan that would bring all of mankind to its knees of repentance and teach it about the vast work on earth of reconciling mankind to God. Man would have the option of being great, powerful, and victorious, or he could choose the easy way of the enemy, which is money, fame, popularity, and imaginary happiness.

You will explore the explosiveness of the Spirit from the beginning to the end— His origin, His mission, His recognition of His love for God and God's people.

THE SOLITUDE OF NEVER

By Patricia E. Davis

In the quietness of the night,

I found *Solitude*

The morning came,

And the sun ran darkness away.

The dew turned from moistness to

Never returning to another day.

Yet, I waited all day for the quietness of

The evening, the stillness, and the

"Solitude of Never"

I pray you find your "Solitude"

HOLY GHOST EMPOWERMENT
TESTIMONY

Many have set out to conquer the unknown, but many have fallen by the way side. The currents of life's issues have sucked them under and the mad clashes of the waves of frustrations and despair have washed them into the deep.

I am here today to thank God, for He has been a Light in my unknown paths of life; He has been my Way; He has been my Captain diverting me from the various currents that would have sucked me under. He has been my Lifeguard directing me from the angry waves, and my Rafter to keep me afloat when I would have gotten carried away into the oceans of afflictions. God has truly received the glory and the honor and He is exalted in that my life has been a test.

I rise not in my own strength but in the power of the Holy Ghost and the anointing of God. These many years of tests have not been good to the flesh, but has engendered growth because of the Holy Spirit within me. The Promised Land was only a few miles away, but on the road there, the enemy diverted me with rocks and blurred-ness, hard knocks, disappointments, disgust, fear, and a desire to regret. However, the Holy Ghost continued to energize me and teach me so that I would be prepared to teach others.

The tears I shed were to wash away my fears, anxieties, hurt and pain, and prepare me to teach others how to go through in spite of the circumstances. The ridicule and persecution were to assist me to rise above the currents to see the glorious fulfillment of the promise that had been established before the foundation of the world. The sickness, the laughter, the confusion, the languish, all was for the perfection of my temple so that I could be touched as Jesus was touched by those who God would bring my way.

The Holy Ghost has taught me how important it is to be available, and obedient to God's command and purpose. Until we get to a point to love God for who He is, not for what He can do for us, our living is in vain. Dying men and women, children, older people, professionals, in need of hope, the harvest is truly plenteous and the laborers are few.

The Holy Spirit calls today, who will go. The challenge is on, the vision is clear, the call is loud, the number is growing, and the Holy Spirit beckons today for workers in God's vineyard. I heard the call of God and through the Holy Spirit, I accepted the call. Yes, it was rocky, lonely, many uncertain days and nights, but I stand victorious in God. The Lord did what He said He would do.

The Holy Ghost Explosion was written through the years of preparation, fortification, and now it's show time! This book is a challenge to every believer to pick up the torch. The torch is life, the way is clear. Run! Run! and don't get weary, then walk and don't faint, for God is calling for willing vessels. He has equipped us with everything we need to get the job done by the Holy Spirit who abides in us. If you don't have that explosive power within, you can. Just ask the Holy Spirit to come in and fill you now! If you have the Holy Spirit and you have not employed His service, you can do that now!

There is a greater work to be done and God wants to know He can count on you. The rewards are great, the work is tremendous, and the load is easy with dependency on God. God is great and greatly to be praised. He is awesome, marvelous, gracious, merciful, and His grace is extended forever.

────────────── CHAPTER 1 ──────────────

THE ORDER REVEALED

God is the Father and the Head of all existence. Jesus Christ is His Son and elder brother of the body of Christ (the Church) and the Holy Spirit or (Holy Ghost) is our Comforter, Teacher and Guide. The only way we can understand and bring ourselves into the presence of the Godhead is :

- We must be born again

- We must possess the Holy Spirit

- We must learn how to pray effectively and in the Holy Spirit

- We must learn how to praise God to get His attention, His action and to receive His Favor.

When new birth occurs, there is a hunger and thirst to be filled with God's Spirit. When we enter into praise and then prayer, the results of these applicable principles will bring an abundant and creative lifestyle. There have been many concepts about the Holy Ghost or the Holy

Spirit. There are questions that have resounded throughout the years. Why do I need to receive the Holy Ghost? Is the Holy Ghost and the Holy Spirit the same? How do I develop the Holy Ghost? You will find answers to the above questions and more as you begin to read *Holy Ghost Explosion.*

The Holy Ghost has been referred to as an "it" in many cases, but the Holy Ghost is a person and is the third person of the Godhead and plays an intricate part in the lives of every believer. In Romans 1:20, Paul states, "The invisible things of him from the creation of the world are clearly seen, being understood by the things that are made, even his eternal power and Godhead," In Colossians 2:2, Paul states "For in him dwelleth all fullness of the Godhead bodily." Therefore, the Spirit is not a separate entity but an intricate part of the Godhead.

You may better understand this concept by looking at a family. There is a Father, who is the head of the household. The Father designates certain responsibilities to the Mother who is the helpmeet of the Father who is her husband, and the Mother in turn passes on responsibilities to the child or children. Each member of the family has a first name but by marriage or birth they take on the name of the Father.

When we accept Christ as our personal Savior, we keep our natural name, but we inherit access to the spiritual characteristics of our Father. From a natural point of view, children that are born have to learn to walk, to talk and to think. As born again believers, we have that responsibility, but it is accomplished through the Holy Ghost. Because the Holy Ghost is a Person as we are in the Spirit, He can identify with each of us on our own level. The Holy Ghost is knowledge and in 2 Corinthians 2:10-11, we see that *"God hath revealed [hidden wisdom] unto us by His Spirit: for the Spirit searcheth all things, yea, the deep things of God. For what man knoweth the things of a man save the spirit of man which is in him, even so the things of God knoweth no man, but the Spirit of God."*

In Nehemiah 9:20, it is stated that *"Thou gavest also thy good spirit to instruct them, and withheldest not thy manna from their mouth, and gavest them water for their thirst.*" In 1 Corinthians 2:13, The Holy Ghost is identified by the Language that is spoken, "*Which things also we speak, not in the words, which the Holy Ghost teaches: comparing spiritual things with spiritual.*" In Romans 8:27, we see that the Spirit searcheth the hearts and knoweth what is the mind of the Spirit because He maketh intercession for the saints according to the will of God.

We must keep in mind that because the Holy Ghost is a person, He has a will as we do. His will is to be obedient to God and assist with the fulfillment of God's plan. In 1 Corinthians 12:11, we read "But all these (gifts) worketh that one and the self same Spirit, dividing to every man severally as he will." The Holy Ghost could not move freely in His guiding, teaching, and comforting without love. God is love and the Holy Ghost must be love, and exemplify love in every aspect. In John 3:16, the Holy Ghost possesses the characteristics of God. "For God so loved the world that he gave his only begotten Son." The Holy Ghost will continue to carry out His responsibility of the Triune as He gives of Himself through Love.

In John 4:34, Jesus lets us know that His meat (work, job, responsibility) is "to do the will of him that sent me, and to finish his work." The Holy Ghost has a work that is only set forth by God through Jesus Christ. In Romans 8:26, the Holy Ghost intercedes, *"Likewise the Spirit also helpeth our infirmities: for we know not what we should pray for as we ought, but the Spirit itself maketh intercession for us with groanings which cannot be uttered."* In John 16:13, the Holy Ghost guides us into all truth and does not speak of Himself but His job is to speak only what He hears and to show us all things.

Do we become wonders when we possess the Holy Ghost? No! We are still in the flesh and our personalities or bodies remain the same, but our spirits, our souls are changed. We actually receive a Spiritual transformation. There is a new mindset, and a greater determination to walk in the will of God and to do the work assigned to each of us. We cannot become tied and give up when faced with life's challenges because the Holy Ghost is at work to assist us.

In 1 Corinthians 2:10, the Spirit searches the deep things so He can reveal to us. We are no longer babes in Christ when we receive the Spirit. Our bodies may get tired but our Spirit continues to be refreshed. When faced with life's challenges, the Holy Ghost reveals to us the solution or comforts us until we come out of the situation.

Many people want the Spirit to be a shield against trouble. That is not His purpose. In fact, Jesus gives us a clear understanding when He explains in John 14:16 that He will "pray the Father, and He shall give you another Comforter." Furthermore, Jesus declared in John 16:33, "in the world ye shall have tribulations." Tribulation is guaranteed. So to strengthen the saints — not shelter — the Holy Spirit is sent.

We cannot make it in this new realm of salvation without teaching. Jesus taught by word, example, and life style to prepare the disciples for His departure and the work that they would inherit. When we receive the Holy Ghost, there are many things we don't understand about God's Word, God's plan for our lives, why things happen to us and the list goes on. However, the Holy Ghost, through the Word of God, is our Teacher.

For, in John 14:26, the Holy Ghost has been sent from God in Jesus name to teach us all things, and to bring all things to our remembrance. It is very important to have daily devotion of reading and studying the Word of God so the Holy Ghost can be kept busy teaching. The Word brings anointing, power, and the completion of God's will in our lives. In order to be a productive saint, we must have the Word taught to us by the Holy Ghost who daily brings fresh manna.

A child who is disobedient to his or her parents may cause the parents to grieve. They have such great aspirations for that child and they only want the best. The Holy Ghost is the same, in that, He is a person. When we are disobedient to the will of God and don't adhere to the voice of the Holy Ghost directing us, it grieves the Holy Ghost.

"Let no corrupt communication proceed out of your mouth, but that which is good to the use of edifying that it may minister grace unto the hearers. And grieve not the Holy Spirit of God whereby ye are sealed unto the day of redemption" (Eph. 4:29,30).

The works of the Holy Ghost are many. Sometimes, we become tired or depressed and feel that we are alone. We begin to surmise in our minds that if the Spirit was real, or if we really had the Spirit, then this would not be happening to us. We must take a serious examination of our self and not find ourselves in the mindset of our forefathers. We should never become so bitter that we allow ourselves to despise the Holy Ghost.

"He that despised Moses' law died without grace under two or three witnesses: Of how much sorer punishment, suppose ye, shall he be thought worthy, who hath troddeth under foot the Son of God and hath counted the blood of the covenant, wherewith he was sanctified, an holy thing, and hath done despite unto the Spirit of grace?" (Heb. 10:28, 29)

The Holy Ghost is on assignment and must fulfill the work the Father has given. Remember, The Holy Ghost is a person and can be resisted, lied to, and blasphemed. In Acts 7:51, we see support of the Holy Ghost resisted and in Acts 5:3, the Holy Ghost was lied to. The consequence is fatal when we lie to the Holy Ghost. God's

mercy is everlasting and His Grace is extended to all mankind, however, blasphemy against the Holy Ghost shall
not be forgiven unto men (Matt. 12:31).

We are striving to be like our Father and our elder
brother, Jesus, but we must possess the same divine characteristics as they do. These characteristics come only
from the Holy Ghost. The characteristics of the Holy
Ghost are eternal (Heb. 9:14), Omniscient (1 Cor. 2:10-
11), Omnipotent (Micah 3:8; Job 33:4) and the Spirit of
Truth and of Love (2 Tim. 1:7) The saints have inherited
so much through the Adoption. We must grasp the fact
that when we receive the Holy Ghost, we have the assurance that, when we die, our soul (Spirit) lives eternally.
Because the Spirit is in us, we have power. We can exemplify truth and love and the revelation of the Spirit who
searcheths all things. When Jesus departed to return to His
Father, He promised to send the Comforter—His Spirit—
so we would not be left alone to be defeated by the enemy.

The Holy Ghost has been in existence before the
conception of mankind. He was the third party of the Trinity and positioned Himself for the empowerment of man-

kind. In the Old Testament, we see the Holy Ghost at work in the Creation. In Genesis 1:2, we see the Spirit of God moving the waters and in Job 33:4, the Spirit helped in the creation of Man.

Although the Spirit needed no help, His performance, the activity in the old was proclaimed by prophets through the Spirit. The Spirit spoke through Noah and he proclaimed it was going to rain, and it did. The Holy Ghost spoke of His coming work in the Christian age, and He is hereby working untiringly to complete this task of assisting every believer that posses Him to find purpose and complete it.

──────────────CHAPTER 2 ──────────────

ATTRIBUTES OF THE HOLY GHOST

In chapter one, we recognized the Holy Spirit is not an "it," He is a person just as we are, in that, He can be identified with many characteristics. In Acts 1:8, the Holy Ghost brings forth His *Attribute of Power.* When He indwells a believer, He brings power to witness. In Acts 2:1, His *Attribute of Unity* is displayed, for we read, "When the day of Pentecost was fully come, they were all with one accord, in one place." The Holy Ghost does not affiliate with unbelievers nor those that bring confusion and are in the wrong place. Therefore, we see in Acts 2:4, the Holy Ghost displays the *Attribute of Organization.* "And they were all filled with the Holy Ghost, and began to speak with other tongues, as the Spirit gave them utterance."

The world continues to promote the educated and there is nothing wrong with that. However, education without the Spirit is void. In Acts 2:6, we see the Holy Ghost confounding all in attendance. There were many

Jews, devout men out of every nation under heaven, but when it was noised abroad and the multitude came together, they were confounded in that every man heard them speak in his own language.

We must come up to this level of the Spirit, and when we do, we shall possess the *Attributes of Amazement* and marvel which was exhibited in Acts 2:7. *"And they were all amazed and marveled saying one to another, Behold are not all these which speak Galileans?"* When we exemplify the attributes as we should, it causes many to marvel and be amazed at our life style, at our job performance, our church performance and our witnessing ability. We can no longer say, "I am weak, I wish I could, or I don't know how." God has provided a part of Himself to be implanted into mankind thereby giving us the power to do, the ability to bring organization in a confused situation, the power for better performance in what ever we are to do.

Around Christmas, birthdays, and anniversaries, we look for gifts. We even get upset if we don't get a gift or a call on these very special days. How many look forward to the day of Pentecost in our lives. How many, with anticipation and excitement ask God for the gift of the Holy Ghost.

In Acts 2:38, there is a pattern for this gift. During Christmas, people are at their best. They say good words—even to people they don't like. With a birthday, people prepare for their guests. There are certain foods prepared, the house is cleaned, all in expectation of a great outcome.

We, too, must make preparations to house the Spirit. Peter gave the prescription to receive the Holy Ghost by letting the people know they had to repent. It was not a performance but they had to ask God to forgive them of their sin and consent to be baptized in the name of Jesus Christ. Then, they would receive the gift of the Holy Ghost.

God's grace is forever extended to the believer by His love that we see when He allowed Jesus Christ to die on the cross in our stead. Yet, Christ did not leave us alone, but sent back the invisible part of Himself to allow mankind to receive this precious gift. The Holy Ghost is such a dynamic person and the attributes are numerous. That's why we could not leave out Acts 2:43, where the Spirit brings anointing and Acts 2:46,47 where the Sprit brings growth. A believer without the anointing cannot be effective.

The anointing is the approval of God and the God-given authority to do His will and to accomplish the designated purpose of our lives. It was not the will of God for man to be lost, so the Holy Ghost is very busy in each believer creating a drive to witness and draw as many to the process of reconciliation. When a believer is filled with the Holy Ghost, the believer sells out, and unifies with other believers, seeks God's will and add to the Church daily such as should be saved.

The Holy Ghost has a personality that exemplifies Knowledge (Prov. 3), Goodness (Neh 9:20), Language (1 Cor. 2:13), Thought (Rom. 8:27) Will (1 Cor. 12:11) and Love (Rom. 15:30) Therefore, erasing all excuses of "I can't, I don't know how." For example, in 1 Corinthians 2:10,11, we see the mission of the Holy Ghost searching all things, and knowing the things of God that no man knoweth. Therefore, if the Spirit is in us, we, too, will search all things and know the things of God. For in Nehemiah 9:20, the personality of the Holy Ghost shows the goodness of God. *"Thou gavest also thy good spirit to instruct them, and withholdest not thy manna from their mouth and gavest them water for their thirst."*

We must erase the concept of thinking things just happen. We get too busy to realize that the Holy Ghost is real and has feelings. We must understand Ephesians 4:30 shows that the Spirit can be grieved. In Hebrews 10:29, the Spirit can be despised, and in Acts 7:51, the Spirit can be resisted. God is all truth and righteousness and knows the heart of man.

When this thought is not perceived and believed in the heart of man, then mankind does not find it difficult to "lie" to the Holy Ghost. In support of this belief, Acts 5:3 shows that Ananias allowed himself to be led to lie to the Holy Ghost. We must realize when we do not tell the truth to the Spirit, we are lying to God. As born again believers, we must not only profess that the Spirit abides in us, but possess the Spirit of Christ.

The Holy Ghost is our avenue to salvation and we must allow Him to lead, guide, and teach us to become perfect. We discover a truth in Matthew 12:31 which reflects the importance of the Holy Ghost. *"All manner of sin and blasphemy shall be forgiven unto men; but the blasphemy against the Holy Ghost shall not be forgiveness to men."* We must realize that the Holy Ghost is one of the Godhead, as it is referenced in Romans 1:20, Col. 2:19, Matthew 18:18-20, 2 Corinthians 13:14, Matthew 3:17 and Genesis 1:26.

When we are filled with the Holy Ghost, we will work. The Holy Ghost performs works such as; Intercession (Rom. 8:26); Guidance (John 16:13); Searching (1 Cor. 2:10); Speaking (1 Tim. 4:10) and Teaching (John 14:26). Looking at the Divine characteristics of the Sprit, we see the Spirit as a part of the Godhead with qualities that are eternal. (Heb. 9:14), Omniscient (1 Cor. 2:10-11) and Omnipotent (Micah 3:8; Job 33:4). We must come to the realization that who God is, Christ is, and who Christ is, the Spirit is, thereby showing us that because of the avenue of adoption, we have eternal life. It must soak in that we are in the image of Christ, and we can do all things through Christ which strengthens us. We can no longer see as others, but our perspective is on a higher plane and our direction is geared to a level of complexity and over whelming victory.

The Holy Ghost is here to stay and His assignment is to dwell in us and empower us. He has a vast responsibility and has been called by many names. He is also called the "Spirit of Truth" and the "Spirit of Love." (1 John 5:6; 2 Tim. 1:7). The Holy Ghost is a divine personality with personal attributes which allows Him to be very active in the believer's life. Will you allow Him to be active in yours?

CHAPTER 3

WHO IS THE HOLY GHOST?

Sometimes, people have a preconceived idea that the Holy Ghost is some type of weird entity that does bodily harm. Many may refer to the Holy Ghost as "wind," "breath," "soul," or "heart." The purpose of the Holy Ghost is to endow God's people with special abilities and gifts such as Jesus had. The same Spirit that descended in a bodily shape like a dove upon Jesus is the same spirit that was recorded in Acts on the day of Pentecost (Luke 3:22). The Spirit descending was symbolic of the fullness of the divine power with which Jesus was endowed as well as other believers that would follow.

The three aspects of the Holy Ghost are power, strength, and aid. The power was experienced on the day of Pentecost as recorded in Acts 2, the strength of the Holy Ghost was for the Church and the aid or guidance for evangelism. We as born again believers should not be weakened by our environment or daily circumstances. We must be encouraged to know the effectiveness of the Holy Ghost and allow Him to have preeminence in our lives.

The Holy Ghost, or Spirit, represents the new age that depicts the law of Christ which replaced the law of Moses and the penalty of death. We are now living in the age of God's divine Grace and Mercy. We have the guidance of the Spirit, the comfort of the Spirit, the direction of the Spirit and the avenue of life rather than death.

In order to receive the Holy Ghost, there is preparation. The people who should receive the Holy Ghost are those who seek Him (Acts 8:15). Those who hear the Word, those are children of God. Those who are sons and daughters (Rom. 8:16, Gal. 4:6). Because God is an inclusive Father, He allows His Spirit to come into every man, woman, and child (1 Cor. 12:11; Acts 16:18)

Today, many people have drifted from reality to fallacy. There is very little significance of the baptism in the eye of modern man. The technological society has gone on a spree of "I can" with the computers and all the mechanical avenues that simplify life. However, the significance of receiving the Spirit is linked between Christ and His church.

Christ knew we would need a Comforter, and empowerment to exist in this present world. When the Spirit is received, there is joy and gladness, even in our testing times. Along with the Spirit comes the Fruit of the Spirit (Gal. 5:22-26). The significance of receiving the Spirit is to help us to be unselfish and to be powerful. In conclusion, the significance of receiving the Holy Ghost is our guarantee of the fullness of salvation.

There should never be a fear in receiving the Holy Ghost, for perfect love casteth out fear. (1 John 4:18). The Holy Ghost is a precious gift from God, and He should be accepted in all humility and honor. It's a privilege for born again believers to be chosen by God for Him to pour out a portion of Himself into each that would receive.

Mankind has continued to drift from the guidance and purpose of God, but the Holy Ghost continues to convert men and women and children so that favor with God may be given. Who is the Holy Ghost? The Holy Ghost is a converter of mankind (John 16:8-11). He reproves sin through the Word of God, righteousness, and judgment. Also, in Psalm 19:7, the Holy Ghost shows Himself as converting the soul. In John 17:17 the

Holy Ghost sanctifies them through truth. In Romans 10:17 faith is given. In 2 Timothy 3:15 wisdom is given unto salvation. In James 1:21, souls are saved.

The workings of the Holy Ghost are multiple and cause a freshening, a revitalization of the born again believer. In all aspects, the work of the Holy Ghost continues in James 1:21 where our souls are saved and in John 8:32. We are set free by knowing the truth, and in 2 Timothy 1:10 life and immortality has been brought to light through the Gospel. We as believers should be rejoicing at the completed work of Christ.

In Christ's death, there was an end to the law and an ushering in of the abundance of God's grace, God's mercy, and His everlasting, divine protection. Because of Christ's resurrection, His ever abiding Spirit, the Holy Ghost in Acts 20:32, was sent back to assist us with the word of grace which is able to build us up and give us an inheritance among all them which are sanctified. In Acts 2:37-38, we see the Holy Ghost working to convert all of those that were pricked in their heart. As a born again believer, there must be a pricking, a hunger and a thirst to gravitate to a new freshness in life.

Because of the inquisitive nature, the instructions were given to "Repent and be baptized." The Holy Ghost will only convert a broken spirit—one who asks God to come in and change the heart, the soul and rid the old nature. The avenue of baptism is an open showing of what has taken place within. There are stages in the development of our lives.

When we are old enough to decide, we must make a choice to live for God or not. Our choice is influenced by our parental Biblical teachings. Once our spirit is enhanced and our mind comprehends, we are able, by the unction of the Holy Ghost, to repent and ask God to come into our lives. A Christian is one who is Christ-like, but a Saint is one who is totally striving to live a sinless life and walk in the image of Christ as much as the Spirit within is in control.

The Holy Ghost comes into one's life by invitation and leads, sanctifies (2 Thes. 2:13), intercedes (Rom. 8:26-27), bears witness (Rom. 8:16), empowers (Eph. 3:16), and comforts (John 14:26). There should be an expectation of joy in the midst of sadness; peace in the midst of confusion; and solutions in the midst of distress. The power of God is working in us and through us thereby allowing the power of the Holy Ghost to make us victors. We no longer have to have a defeated life and succumb to the enemies tactics. We are more than conquerors and we are victorious through Christ Jesus.

As recorded in Joel 2:28-29 and Isaiah 61:1, It was foretold of the pouring of the Holy Ghost on all flesh and the Spirit would be with the Messiah as well. As creatures of God, we have the opportunity to reside in this prophecy and in the fulfillment of the power of God. The works of the Holy Ghost are revealed in the New Testament letters with reference to the name Holy Ghost 57 times and reference to the Spirit and His work 69 times. The Spirit is mentioned in the 21 epistles 132 times. The importance of these recordings is to give us, as born-again believers, evidence that the Spirit (Holy Ghost) is real and does work.

Jesus lived on earth and was endowed with power from above by His Father to do a work, and we have that same advantage. We see the power of Jesus recorded in the listings to encourage us in our living. Luke 1:35 states He was begotten of the Spirit; John 5:19 states He would do nothing of Himself; and 1 Timothy 3:16 states He was justified in the Spirit and Luke 4:1 states He was led by the Spirit and Rom. 8:1; 1:4 states He was raised by the Spirit.

In Romans 8:15,16, we are no longer in bondage because we receive the Spirit of adoption which bears witness with our Spirit that we are the children of God. The power, the anointing, the pleasures of all heaven belong to us, and we must learn how to receive from our Father in portion of our maturity.

Who is the Holy Ghost? The Holy Ghost is not to be played with or thought to be called upon when we need temporal things. He is not to be played with or taken lightly, but He is the all knowing Spirit of His Father—God. The Holy Ghost is an active third person of the Trinity and is purposed to bring reconciliation to all mankind by God's power being activated in all born again believers.

When we look at the activity of the apostles, we see a dynamic performance of miracles. The Holy Ghost moved through them by Acts of power, assurance (John 14: 16-18), guidance (Acts 2:42) and gifts (Acts 2:43). The apostles exemplified the power of the Holy Ghost by speaking and writing the inspired Word (John 16:13-14) by doing miracles to confirm the Word (Heb. 2:3-4) and by bestowing miraculous gifts on others and by laying on of their hands (Acts 8:17; 19:6).

The Word is powerful and our Faith brings this Word off the printed page to form the power of the Holy Ghost within us. Who is the Holy Ghost? He is our instructor, our road map to God, and our Helper in realizing our purpose. Our power is in the belief and obedience of the Word. The apostles were so effective in that they allowed the Spirit to dictate to them through their inner being which allowed them to speak what the Spirit said and what God said (1 Cor. 2:13; Matt. 10:20).

Who is the Holy Ghost? He is everything that we ever will need to live on this earth and complete the task that has been assigned to us.

CHAPTER 4

THE GIFTS OF THE SPIRIT

A spiritual gift is something given or bestowed with special qualifications granted by the Spirit to every believer for empowerment to serve within the framework of the body of Christ. As children of God, we all are given a gift or gifts. Our gifts are assigned to us when we are born into the family of God by the Holy Spirit.

The word *pneumatic* is used to describe the spiritual concept which refers to the source of gifts as the Holy Ghost. The usual word is *charisma.* (plural *charismata*, as in Rom. 12:6) which means gift of Grace. The source of the gifts of the Spirit are the special grace of the Holy Ghost, the nature of the Holy Ghost, spiritual ability, endowment, power, the purpose of the Holy Ghost, and the service, or ministry to edify saints.

Gifts are universal in that everyone of us is given a gift by Gods grace according to the measure of the gift of Christ (Eph. 4:7). However, the manifestation of the Spirit is given to every man to profit withal (1 Cor. 12:7). Christ promised not to leave us unequipped when He departed.

Therefore, the gifts along with the Holy Ghost were given for the perfecting of the saints, the work of the ministry, and for the edifying of the body of Christ.

When we look at the gift of teaching, we see that this gift does not function by itself. Teaching is accompanied by a "gift" or "gifts" and talents. Many times, gifts and talents are confused as to what is what and who possess what. Let's look at the distinctive characteristic of each. The gift of teaching is the supernatural ability to explain clearly and apply effectively the truth of the Word of God. The gift of teaching functions in the supernatural by the Spirit of God, who operates decently and in order, building His gift with supernatural power upon the foundation of the talent already there.

TALENTS VS. GIFTS

The distinguishing factor of talent is that any unique talent is present from natural birth and operates through common grace in society. It is evident that talent is communicated in any subject and often yields just understanding of a topic. A talent has techniques and methods that depend on natural power which instructs, inspires, or entertain on a natural level. However, a gift is present from spiritual birth and operates through special grace and the Church. The gift communicates biblical truth and prepares for involvement and obedience through spiritual abilities and spiritual endowment to build up the saints. With the gift of teaching there is clear communication, effective application and a body of truth.

The lists of Gifts may be found in the following biblical passages:

Romans 12:3-8—*Prophecy, Ministering (Helps), Teaching, Exhorting, Giving, Government (Ruling) and Showing Mercy.*

1 Corinthians 12:8-12, 28-30—*Word of Wisdom, Word of Knowledge, Faith, Healing, Miracles, Prophecy, Discernment, Tongues, Interpretation, Apostleship, Teaching, Ministration (Helps), and Government (Ruling).*

Ephesians 4:ll—*Apostleship, Prophecy, Evangelism, Pastoring, and Teaching*

The Classification of Gifts are placed in the following listed categories:

Speaking—*Apostleship, Prophecy, Evangelism, Pastoring, Teaching, Exhorting, Word of Knowledge, Word of Wisdom, Tongues and Interpretation.*

Ministering—*Serving, Ministration (Helps), Hospitality, Giving, Government (Ruling), Showing Mercy, Faith, Discernment, Miracles, and Healing.*

Signifying—*Miracles, Healing, Tongues, and Interpretation.*

The Holy Ghost knows which gifts are needed, whom to fill with these gifts and where to provide these gifts. The Church cannot be totally effective without the operations of the gifts. The gifts are used for the enhancement and development of ministry.

MINISTERING GIFTS

The Gifts of Helps (1 Corinthians 12:28) carries the meaning of assistance, lending a hand. This gift is the Spirit given ability to serve the Church in any supporting role, usually temporal, though sometimes spiritual. The gift enables one to serve joyfully and diligently wherever and whenever required.

The Gift of Government (Rom. 12:8) deals with ruling and leadership. The verb *Proistemi* means to stand over, place over, set over, superintend, preside, and is translated rule. The word *kuberneis* is used for the gift of government (master) steersman, and may be referenced in Acts 27:11 and ship master in Revelation 18:17. The word *hegeomai* means go before, lead, be a leader, rule, command, have authority over, governor, ruler and reference may be found in Acts 7:10. The gift of government may be shown by the spiritual authority expressed in wisdom, tact, humility, and service. The gift of government is the Spirit-given ability to preside, govern, plan, organize, and administer with wisdom, and fairness. The gift of government is exemplary in humility, service, confidence ease and efficiency.

The Gift of Faith is a Spirit given ability to see something that God wants done and to sustain unwavering confidence that God will do it regardless of seemingly insurmountable obstacles. The gift of Faith makes the impossible possible; believes that God wants it; begins thanking in advance and announcing it will be so; turns vision into reality; knows when helpless situations are not hopeless and does the impossible.

The Gift of Discernment is a special ability to distinguish between the Spirit of truth and the spirit of error. The gift of discernment can distinguish between that which is raised up by God and that which pretends to be. One who possess this gift has the ability to unmask Satan's trickery, to detect false teachings, and to ferret (search) out false teachers. This gift has the ability to spot a phony before others see through the phoniness. The Bible speaks of many falsities that would surface in the last days. We must be wise and pray for a deeper discerning spirit to detect the anti-Christ, false prophets, false apostles, tares, wolves in sheep clothing and the unclean spirits (Matt. 16:17; Acts 5:1-10).

The Gift of Miracles (1 Corinthians 12:10, 28) is an event of supernatural power. This gift accompanies the servant of the Lord to authenticate the divine commission.

This gift involves the Spirit-given power to perform an act contrary to natural law. (Mark 2:12; Luke 5:4-9) A miracle exalts God in His highest authoritative power of abolishing ordinary laws of nature and doing the extraordinary for His glory.

The Gift of Healing is the ability to intervene in a supernatural way as an instrument for the curing of illness and the restoration of health (Matt. 9:35; Acts 6:8). This gift does not heal every illness and does not depend on the sick people's faith, nor account for all healing, but works so that God can be manifested (John 9:1-3). In the ministry of healing, healing is initiated by the sick, and the application of oil is used as the sacred symbol of the Spirit. The word anoint in Greek is *Chiro—Christ* meaning anointed or anoint sacredly. *Aleipho* means to oil, applying or rubbing oil on the body. The types of healing are prayer, bodily healing, and forgiveness.

The Gifts of Tongues is to authenticate the Gospel messengers. The word *glossolalia* (speaking in tongues) can bring clarity to those seeking understanding of tongues or interpretation. Tongues should not be spoken at the same time because it becomes confusing and takes away from the real message of God. We must understand tongues are spoken, they are not biblical methods of Christian growth nor the exclusive domain of Christianity, nor the sign of maturity or spirituality, nor a church building gift, nor the test of ecumenicity (universal, inhabit)

The Gift of Interpretation is the ability to translate by someone who did not know the language. In order for you to discover your gift or gifts, it is suggested that you pray and seek God; go to work and get involved in various parts of the ministry; desire spiritual gifts (1 Cor. 12:31); dedicate your self to God and His purpose for your life; develop your talent or talents; delight yourself in God, His work and His people and consider spiritual guidance from pastors, or spiritual leaders, and then adhere.

THE SPEAKING GIFTS

The Apostolic Gift is associated with one who states their apostleship. The word apostle occurs 75 times in the New Testament with explanation of one who states they have personally been with Jesus from the beginning and has received a personal call from Christ and has witnessed the resurrection or has laid the doctrinal foundation of the church, or has laid the structural foundation of the church, and has the power to work miracles. An apostle's call gives hope that he too will sit on 12 thrones judging the 12 tribes of Israel (Luke 22:29). An apostle believes that his name will be inscribed on the 12 foundations of the New Jerusalem. (Rev. 21:14)

Some debate that there is no difference between an apostle and a missionary. A missionary is one who is sent (rooted in the Latin—"to send"), and an apostle is rooted in the Greek "to send." They both exemplify the same duties, but in a different capacity and quantity. They have the ability to serve in another culture as well as planting goals, conversion, baptism, growth, and the organized fellowship. Wait! Do we get bogged down with titles, or do we lock arms, minds and visions and go in the power of God to do a great work? Think about it! A "missionary," a "Bishop," it's just a title. The work and the purpose accomplished is what makes you; and God rewards you for the labor of love.

The Gift of Prophecy derives from the English word prophet which comes from a Greek word composed of two parts which mean literally—foretell. A prophet is God's spokesman and receives revelation from God by dreams, visions, verbal communication (often used a graphic object lesson to emphasize the message), warn, exhort, promote righteousness that was historical, practical and relevant to contemporary conditions.

For example, Agabus, in Acts 11:27, 28 and 1 Corinthians 14:3-4, refers to edifying. This prophetic gift encouraged, and comforted as well. We must state that the gift of prophecy is the Holy Ghost-given ability to proclaim the written Word of God with clarity and to apply it to a particular situation with a view to correct or edify.

The Gift of Evangelism is not recorded as a gift per se but does appear in the English language in the 17th century and occurs only 3 times in the New Testament. Those references are: Acts 21:8; Ephesians 4:11, and 2 Timothy 4:5. The gift of evangelism may be defined as the proclamation of good news regarding salvation. An evangelist may exercise the gift of teaching in such a demonstrative way that the teaching arouses people to respond to the claims of Christ in conversion and in discipleship.

One must understand that evangelism is more than screaming and running from place to place to receive a big check. Evangelism has many categories and when used in the area of its position, the church, and membership can grow and benefit. The types of evangelism are: Bible distribution, breakfasts (prayer, foreign mission, etc.), child evangelism, college campus, door-to-door calling, drug rehabilitation, films, home Bible studies, hospital visitation, letter writing, literature, open air, phone, prison, radio, rescue missions, T.V., tracts, and visitation.

The Gift of Shepherding is associated with the "Pastor" which occurs once in the New Testament (Eph. 4:11). It refers to an office in the church (bishop and elder). The nature of the gift of shepherding is to guide (Is. 40:11), to feed with knowledge and understanding (Jer. 3:15), and to protect from hostile influence (Acts 20:28).

The Holy Ghost presents so many opportunities for us to use the power within to develop and to strengthen the body of Christ. As believers, we must seek God to find out what our gift or gifts are and begin studying to perfect them so that we can be a blessing to Gods people and ourselves.

The Gift of Exhortation is to comfort, console, entreat, implore and counsel. The Holy Ghost is called the Comforter and encourager (John 14:16), and the Lord Jesus is called our Advocate (1 John 2:1). Comforter and Advocate could be translated as *paraclete* in that they both are with us to help us along the way. The gift of exhortation involves the supernatural ability to come along side to help, to strengthen the weak, reassure, console, and encourage (Acts 14:21,22).

The Gift of Knowledge is the Charisma which enables the believer to search, systematize, and summarize the teachings of the Word of God. This gift also brings illumination of God's thoughts not discoverable by human reason (2 Peter 3:18).

The Gift of Wisdom is the ability to apply knowledge to perplexing situations thereby weighing the realness of the situation. The gift of Wisdom exercises spiritual insight into the right and wrong avenues of a difficult situation to bring a positive result.

The Gift of Hospitality is referenced in Rom. 12:13 and its base word is "hospital." It is derived from the ancient travelers, whether pilgrims or businessman, who were on the road and had not rested for many days. Religious leaders set up international guest houses in the fifth century and called these rest areas " hospice" from *hospes* (the Latin word for guests-haven). Therefore, the gift of hospitality is that supernatural ability to provide an open house and warm welcome for those in need of food, lodging, and other needs.

The Gift of Giving involves giving with simplicity and singleness of mind. There is no pretense, but an involvement of giving freely with delight, liberal, and not grudging or of necessity (2 Cor. 9:7). The gift of giving involves knowing that the avenue of giving will allow the work of God to be promoted. The born again believer learns there is joy in giving and delights in giving out of love. This freedom of giving results in liberality which many cannot have unless it is pursued. This liberality is only God given.

The Gift of Mercy is the Holy Ghost-guided ability to manifest practical, compassionate, cheerful, love toward suffering members of the body of Christ (Rom. 12:8). How can we go out and witness, feed the hungry, and minister to a dying world if we forget to minister to our own brothers and sisters. The Holy Ghost assists us with focus and intent as well as focus and purpose. The gift of showing mercy goes beyond feeling and convenience, it reaches out when we don't feel like it, or feel that the person deserves mercy.

The Holy Ghost opens our eyes to see where God has brought us from and how God's mercy saved us, helped us, cared for us, and continues to reach out to us in our various situations. Many gravitate to what they consider the "big" gifts where they can approach the platform, but how many gravitate to the gift of mercy. It is the gifts that seem small and have no glamour that have the biggest rewards.

CHAPTER 5

GETTING AN UNDERSTANDING

This chapter is designed to assist you in understanding many words you read in your Bible study or Greek and Hebrew words that you may not know. This chapter will broaden your understanding in your daily devotion, in your church messages and in your study relationship between you and God.

You must know that the Holy Ghost brings all things to our remembrance, but we must put something there in order for it to be brought to us. Studying is very important along with prayer and praise. However, to enhance our delivery, we go beyond the mere two or three letter words that shows lack of maturing in the depth, height, and breadth of God's Word. The list of vocabulary words are designed for your study and intermingling of your reading to assist you in getting a better understanding of God's Word.

Christian maturity is an advancement such as levels of grades in school. When you learn the first grade curriculum, you advance to the second, then third, and so on.

In this Christian walk, we advance to grades or levels in our lives. We go up the ladder of success based on the amount of time, and development of the godly principles we learn. We learn these principles to provide a foundation of godly living—a godly life style.

Patience—The ability of learning to wait through your trials and tribulations.

Grace—The graciousness of God to provide unlimited favor, blessings to mankind.

Experience—The knowledge and wisdom acquired by the daily things that one undergoes in this life.

Glory—The ever presence of God in all of His attributes of goodness, grace, and mercy that is manifested to the believer, most of the times, in praise.

Commendeth—An order, a decree of worthiness placed upon us.

Sin—That which goes against the laws or will of God.

Law—The ordinances of God that gave man the plan of living, but yet showed the sins of all mankind.

Whisperer—One who gossips, one who secretly delivers information, whether true or false, to slander ones character or name.

Backbiter—One who goes behind peoples' backs to spread untrue information or to defame character.

Proud—As stated in Proverbs, this is one who has an arrogant behavior, to present ones self as better than others.

Justification—No one can bring this privilege to man but God who declares us good, right, only through the blood of Jesus Christ by faith.

Redemption—The avenue of giving money, or something dear to bring back that which was lost. Jesus was that avenue by way of His shed blood for the remission of sin.

Propitiation—The act of removing wrong and making it right, restoring the broken and damaged fellowship between God and mankind.

Sanctification—The sinner had no hope but through the love of God who declared man holy through the works of the Holy Ghost to keep us, once we were saved, free from all corruption and to set us aside for the work of God.

Righteousness of the Father—He is the righteous governor of all creatures, and He gives punishment as well as rewards.

Righteousness of Christ—Depicted in His birth, death, and resurrection which shows His faithfulness, holiness and justice.

Gospel—Good news presented to the world through the preaching of the disciples regarding the birth, death, and resurrection of Jesus.

Vial—A flask or bottle. (Rev. 5:8) holds the prayers of the Saints.

Knop—Ornamenting candlesticks in the tabernacle. Ornaments carved on walls of Solomon's temple. 1 Kings 6:18

Thelo—One's emotion that brings a specific desire.

Boulomai—One's reason that develops a desire.

Splogchnizomai—The Lord Jesus was moved with compassion, the Greek word moved with compassion.

Evagglion—The deliverance of good news that brings a message.

Christos—Jesus, the anointed One

Hodos—A road that is frequently traveled.

Homologes—To confess, to speak the same of clarity.

Agape—Comes from the heart, the inner being of the people—love.

Eudokeo—To have found favor, or well pleasing in the sight of God.

Disbolos—Devil—defame, or accuse.

Peirazomai—Tempted, to become weak and yield.

Didasko—To instruct or teach

Didache—Belief, doctrine

Exousia—The power, authority

Epitimao—The avenue to rebuke, to bring to silence, correction.

Aphiemi—depart, leave

───────── CHAPTER 6 ─────────

PRAYER

Prayer is God's way of communicating with mankind and man being able to speak to God. The opportunity and privilege of talking with God is limitless. Prayer is conversation with God which brings about communication between man and God to display an earnest request with a humble entreaty made to God. In our approach to God in prayer, God shows His great love for mankind thereby allowing us in prayer to formulate and manifest our devotion to Him which causes God to grant that which we desire. Remember, we can only desire what God has placed in our Spirit because God has already made it available for reception.

We may conclude that prayer is the desire for the advance and consummation of God's work among men, and the expression of submission to His will as we praise His holy name. How can you begin to pray? The baby is crying, you have a mile-long to-do list for the day, the job, the activities for the church and the children, and the list goes on. Wait! Let's look at the importance of this great avenue that has been afforded by God.

How do we effectively enter into His presence and receive those requests and communicate with Him? We cannot just jump right in with "God I need..." or "I want..." or "help me...". One must begin with praise and worship in the morning and before going to bed. Once you find out how easy it is, you will extend your prayer time each day and night. Once you become engulfed in His presence, and you begin speaking to God and He to you, you will not want to leave His presence. You will develop a desire, a hunger and thirst to have more time with your Father through the Holy Ghost. Always remember that, sacrifice brings results. When you begin to thank God, lift up your hands in praise, begin saying words such as "thank You Lord", "I love You Lord", "I appreciate You Lord," "There is none like you", and so on, you bring yourself into His presence.

From the beginning of time, man has believed in an elevated being. He often referred to the God of the mountains. This symbolic connotation could have stemmed from the vivid description of Moses that saw the burning bush afar that would not burn and lured him to the mountains with curiosity. Nevertheless, the desire to pursue a higher being and to be in the position of "power seeking" was instilled in man by God.

In 1 Chronicles 29:16, David specifies his desire to build God a house for His holy name. In prayer, you may lift your hand in total surrender to God. God is magnificence and desires the "Thank You, Lord", "I love You", "You are gracious and worthy to be praised," and more. The act of verbal praise brings you into the presence of God's greatness which humbles you with uplifted hands (1 King 8:22), or you may kneel (Ps. 95:6), or lay before Him (Num. 16:22) or cry aloud from your inner being (Ps. 28:2).

In order to pray, you must meet certain prerequisites. In order to condition yourself for prayer, you must have the right attitude and a hunger and thirst for God, more than yourself. You must exemplify pure praise in a state of humility. Your request and supplication must not be selfish, but for the enlistment of God's kingdom and the fulfillment of purpose. There must be a sprinkling of thankfulness in your soul throughout your praying.

We must be grateful for the grace and mercy of God which delivered us through the blood of Jesus. Without God's mercy and grace, we would still be praying to the various gods, or going to the priest to make atonement for our sins. It is through the shed blood of Christ on the cross, that the veil was rent, thereby allowing us freedom to come boldly to the throne of God's grace and mercy. In Hebrews 10:19-21, we are informed that we can enter into the Holy of Holies by the blood.

Christ has given a new way which He has consecrated for us. The veil was rent when He died and bled on the cross. Jesus now stands as the mediator between man and God. We must accept Christ as the High Priest and walk therein. Our prayers are kept in heaven's vial and God hears and sees our every groan. When we can't pray, but are in a moaning posture, we have a vial of prayers, tears, and praise that is recorded in heaven.

It is very important that we know about the beginning of the entrance of our prayers and how we have been afforded the luxury of praying before our Father by ourselves, for ourselves and others. The description of the

"Holy Place" includes the description of the Tabernacle, Table of Show Bread, Golden Candlestick, and the Altar of incense. (See diagram in back of book.)

The Holy of Holies is where the Ark of the Covenant was housed and carried. This place was a structure of wood covered with gold in which there were the tablets of the law, Moses' budding staff, and a pot of manna, which was a special food provided for the Israelites during the exodus from Egypt; it was a white delicious flavored plant of Eastern Mediterranean that amazed all by the time it came, how it came, and the preservation of this manna.

In prayer, the Holy Spirit brings clarity. There is a new language that we now have such, as Abba-Father. The hebrew word *Ab* is the word that Jesus used when He addressed God in prayer (Mark 14:36). We often pray and it seems like we are not getting through. We fall on our knees, we cry, we even lay prostrate before the Lord and there seems to be no answer. This is all good, but prayer begins when man develops a desire for God and a need of God. God hears prayer when man draws nigh to Him (James 4:8).

You must know that God answers every one of our prayers (Heb. 11:6). A surrendered life in Christ makes a successful prayer life possible and brings clarity to our very present situation by the Spirit of Christ. We must totally learn to absent ourselves from our little concepts of power and learn to rely on divine strength for a fruitful, godly life. God answers prayer when there is a continual seeking after the grace and power of God, and praying in the Holy Spirit which helpeth our infirmity (Rom. 8:26, 27). Once the Spirit brings clarity, we know that it is not by might or power but by the Spirit of God.

We now begin our quest to find out why we need the Holy Spirit. We need the Holy spirit because He is our channel to God our Father. He is our mediator and intercessor in that all of our prayers are taken to Jesus by the Spirit to the throne of Divine Grace that our spirit has expressed in prayer. The Spirit interprets what we are trying to say to God and immediately there is an answer. What answer? Yes, No, or Wait. Two of these answers are not what we want to hear but they are good for building patience, character, and teaching us to trust God.

Remember, every sincere prayer offered to God by His faithful children receives an answer from Him. Think efficacy (power to produce intended results; effectiveness). There is nothing too hard for us who posses the Holy Spirit because the God in us has unlimited power. Women should be excited about Christ's liberty. It was recorded that 5,000 men, women, and children were seated and fed. Along with other recordings, it stated that the women only could pray at the foot of the tabernacle. Women were to be seen and not heard. However, when Christ died, shed His blood, and sent His Holy Spirit to comfort all of humanity, everyone who believes, and receives can come boldly to the throne of grace.

Prayer is personal to each believer and through our prayers we learn how to discover the riches of Christ (1 Tim. 6:17). Prayer is tapping into God's riches (*exichniasstos*- Greek) and plugging into the currents of God's power. Prayer sets us free and makes operative the power of God. It is the connecting wire which God uses to transmit His power in our lives and thus enables us to get above and beyond ourselves. Prayer humbles us, cleanse us, and reveals God's purpose to us. In order to strengthen your belief in prayer, hear are a few study passages:

Elijah's prayer at Mount Carmel (1 King 18:36-39)

Hezekiah's prayer for deliverance from the Assyrians (2 Kings 19:15-19)

After studying these scriptures, how has your prayer concept been enhanced? You cannot just begin praying, you must enforce the conditions of acceptable prayer. Each person has worked or is working a job and on that job, there are goals; there are agendas to follow; there are formats to make that establishment a better working organization. In God's kingdom, there are conditions that must be met in order for us to advance to the next level. When you pray, you must apply:

Humility

Sincerity

Fervency—not half hearted, listless, but whole mind, body, and soul projected toward the mind of God.

Persistency (don't give up)

Watchfulness

Thoughtfulness

God living (life style)

Self denial

In accordance with God's will

In the name of Jesus the Christ

Faith

There are three elements of acceptable prayer that we must now examine. The first one is *Communion*. This elements causes us to turn our attention toward God. We block out all things and get alone to hear our Father. The second element is *Petition* which allows us to express our own needs. I know we feel guilty when we pray and don't ask God for the things we need.

We state that God will take care of us, but we must express our need in faith and believe that we have received it. The last element is very important and must be included in order to have effective results. This element of *Intercession* is when we turn our attention toward the needs of others. We forget about ourselves and see the needs of others stronger than our own. Compassion sets in and we see through the eye of God, and we exemplify the love of God.

When we pray, there is a communion between God and us through the adoration and praise, the thanksgiving and the confession. In communion, there is a removal of every barrier between the Christian and God. There is an attitude of complete submission to God. In prayer, we often write down things that we want and prioritize them. The Greek word for petition is *praoseuche* which means making a request or asking, describing the petitionary function of our speaking to God. The Greek word *Deesis* means supplication, need, seeking, asking, entreating. Therefore, when we pray, we seek God.

Should we seek God for blessings? Yes, we should seek God for blessings. What type of blessings should we ask for, and what is the difference in the various types of seeking? Let's address the physical blessings. This blessing is bodily sustenance (Matt. 6:11), and bodily health (Philippians 4:6) and material means to help others (Eph. 4:28). Now, the spiritual blessings emphasize the forgiveness of sins (Matt. 6:12), the power to withstand temptation (1 Cor. 10:13), wisdom (James 1:5), and learning how to exercise faith and love (Mark 9:24). There must be co-operation with God in prayer and we must pray in faith and sincerity to make our prayer effectual. We learn to pray with commitment and develop a hunger to know and accomplish God's will for our lives.

Prayer is great but it is even better when we learn to intercede for others. We pray for others as well as our-selves. In 1 Timothy 2:1, we are exhorted "that supplica-tion, prayers, intercessions, giving of thanks, be made for all men." You may ask the questions of "when and where to pray?"

When—Pray without ceasing (1 Thess. 5:17); Praying always (Col. 1:3); Praying at all seasons (Eph. 6:18) and always to pray and not to faint (Luke 18:1)

Where—any place, because God is omnipresent.

THE ATTITUDE AND SPIRIT OF UNCEASING PRAYER

Prayer never ceases, therefore, the entire life of the faithful saint is an unceasing prayer. The faithful saint prays without ceasing the sense of maintaining an unbroken dependence on God. The practice of unceasing prayer is if you pray much, you will have much power. We must pray in times of sickness, poverty, and sorrow. We must especially pray in times of heath, prosperity, and happiness so that we will stay on the spiritual track and remain focused on our Source—God. We must never forget to begin and end our day with prayer. We must have the Holy Ghost because Romans 8:26-27 states the Holy Ghost helpeth our infirmities, and maketh intercession for us according to the will of God.

When you pray, you must take charge and command in prayer (Matt. 7:7), you must receive encouragement in prayer (Mark 11:24) you must be sincere and know that your prayers are heard and answered (Ps. 10:17). In order to have effective prayer, you must be truthful (Ps. 145:18). You cannot come before God as a liar because He knows who you are and you will only hinder your answered prayer. You must be who you are and know that it is the power of God that can deliver you and this can only be done through prayer (Matt. 6:5,6).

The spirit of humility must be exemplified, for you cannot obtain the effectiveness of your prayer without humbling yourself before God. Jesus did it and we are in His image and we must walk, talk, and believe as He did (James 4:10). We must always pray in the name of Jesus, the Christ (John 16:26). We must always remember the effective prayers are those that ask for what you do not possess, seek for what is not apparent, and knock that obstacles may be removed, deleted, and abolished.

HINDRANCES TO PRAYER

Distractions

Have you ever noticed that when you get ready to pray the phone rings, the child cries, the door bell rings, the pot in the kitchen boils over and the list goes on. You must persevere (1 Peter 4:7).

<u>Disobedience</u>

When you desire to walk with God, carry His anointing, and be trusted with His Word to deliver to His people, you cannot be hindered in your prayer life by disobedience. You cannot be stubborn when the Spirit tells you to confess your sins, and ask for forgiveness, you cannot be disobedient to the Word and will of God yourself when you are expecting God to do wonders in your life through prayer.

<u>Asking amiss</u>

In James 4:3, you must pray for the glorification of God—not for your own glory and proud exposure. When your motive to pray is for material, or temporal and not to glorify God, it is of no avail. Your prayer must be concerned with relieving poor, distressed, and afflicted people. Furthermore, these prayers must come from your heart, not for your carnal appeasement

EXAMPLES OF PRAYER

Read Luke 9:1-7, Matthew 15:29-37 and Luke 9:12, what points do you glean from the various prayers. Study. Look at the call—given assignment, challenge, who received the Glory, what did it take for the answered prayer.

_____

_____

_____

_____

_____

_____

_____

_____

_____

_____

_____

_____

_____

_____

_____

_____

_____

_____

_____

_____

_____

_____

_____

_____

Take time to begin reading and studying the listed books and chapters in the Bible regarding prayer. As you read, list the important facts that relate to the materials that we have already covered and how this study relates to you and can assist you to advance to another level.

I. 1 King 18:36-38

II. 2 Kings 19:15-19

III. Daniel 6:10

IV. Jonah 2:1-2, 7, 10

V. Acts 9:36-40 (Prayer for Dorcas)

VI. Acts 12:5-12 (Prayer for Peter in prison)

CHAPTER 7

How the Holy Ghost Is Operative

We have seen the beginning of the Holy Spirit and have learned how to pray and seek God for His will to be done. We have learned the conditions of prayer, and now, what do we do with all of this knowledge? How is the Holy Ghost operative, in the home and on the job and throughout our lives?

Praise—Psalm 45:17

> Loose shackles
>
> Free minds
>
> Set stage for Receptivity of the Word
>
> Add to the Church such as should be saved
>
> Bind contrary spirits

Sensitivity— Mark 1:41

Ability to discern a need, a contrary spirit, a break through in the service or the deliverance of a soul.

Prayer—Acts 6:4; Acts 12:5; Philippians 4:6

> Pray that contrary spirits be bound.
>
> Pray for the moving of God's presence throughout

every listener.

Pray for the pastor.

Pray for souls to be saved.

Pray the sick to be healed.

Pray for miracles to take place.

Unlimited Flow of Power—Acts 1:8; 2 Timothy 1:7

Release the bound

Set captive free

Insight

The Spirit was, is, and always shall abide, but the introduction of the Spirit now cries out for God's people to rush and seek the fulfilling. The Spirit desires to be a part of God's creation so that we can be comforted, guided, and instructed in order to carry out the mission that God has assigned each of us. The Hebrew word for Spirit is *Ruach* and it means wind, breath, and life created by God. It is the soul or heart (the seat of the intelligence and emotion).

The Spirit is the principles of life which God imparts to man at his beginning. The Spirit endows us with special abilities and gifts such as leadership, craftsman-ship, and wisdom. The Spirit came with power on the day of Pentecost with gifts of healing and prophecy, speaking and interpretation of tongues to strengthen the church in-wardly, to aid in evangelism, and to link between Christ and the Church. The Spirit teaches, guides into truth, brings to remembrance, bears witness, declares things to come, glorifies Christ, takes things that are His and de-clares them, and acts as a conveyor.

The mission of the Spirit is fulfilled in the capacity of comforting and abiding in us forever. However, when God moves, so does the enemy, and there are many that feel, think, and maybe even are told they are spiritual. Let's see the difference between spiritual and spiritualism.

Spiritual—Of the Spirit and soul. Possesses the wisdom, knowledge, faith, healing, miracles, prophecy, discerning of spirits, speaking in tongues, and interpretation of tongues. One who is spiritual knows how to move in and out of the service and areas that God's directs them. They are quiet spoken and humble in their delivery. They seek to please God and not man.

They are always about making a difference for God and giving Him glory and not pulling people to themselves. They love God and His people and put God first, His people and themselves last. They love the work and Word of God and are found studying God's Word, doing His will and giving of themselves, their money, time and efforts for the betterment of God's work, leader, and congregation. They exemplify faith and a life style of prayer and radiance.

Spiritualism—the belief that the dead survive as spirits which can communicate with the living, especially with the help of a medium. For in Roman 1:21-26, because of disbelief, and rebellion, God gave them up and therefore they believed a lie rather than the truth.

There can be no middle ground. You must believe God, Jesus, and the Spirit and allow the power of God to work in you and not play with God. The power and love of God is free and He desires to reconcile mankind to Himself into a perfect state as was before. We cannot allow the enemy to trick us into having some made-up power and prayer, when God offers the real product for free. It is free to us, but Jesus paid the ultimate price once and for all on the cross when He died for us and shed His blood for our redemption.

The power of God can only be used when we love the Word of God, read and study the Word of God, make a stand for what we believe and who we believe in, be authoritative in our presentation, be strong, and exemplify the attitude of power, discernment, be prayerful, be thankful, and recognize God as the Source of our power. Power is only used to set the captive free and to bring glory and admiration to God.

CHAPTER 8

PRAISE

We have heard so many times that the answer is in praise and if we praise God the blessings will come down. It is more than opening our mouths and saying "thank You." We must know the meaning of praise and exercise the factors of praise at all times. When we address praise, it is the honor rendered for worth, approval, laudation, being joyful, giving tribute or homage to God for the many things He has done. Giving thanks for God's mercies and goodness to all mankind.

Let's examine the listed scriptures and see what we mean when we say praise to God.

Exodus 15:2; Judges 5:3; 2 Samuel 22:50; 1 Chronicles 16:9; 1 Chronicles 29:13; Psalm 9:11; 21:13; 22:3; 34:3; Isiaiah 12:14; Jeremiah 51:10; Daniel 4:37; Joel 2:26; Luke 1:46; 2:20; 19:37 and 1 Peter 2:9.

There must be offerings of praise in order to have a solid foundation for praise. The offerings of praise deal with the sincere desire of the worshipper to enter into fellowship with God. (wave offering—Exodus 29:24-28)

We must know that when we praise God, it is because of the following:

Fellowship

To be full of joy

To be illuminated

To come out of darkness

To illuminate someone else

To loose shackles

To bring in the manifestation of the blessings

Let's look at the avenues of praise and worship. A service cannot have the juice and excitement without the tears, the applauds, and the laughter of the mixed congregation. The praise and worship may be heightened by the studying of the listed scriptures: Psalm 26:12; 35:18; 68:26; 89:5; 100:4; 107:32; Acts 2:47; 16:25; Ephesians 5:19; Hebrews 2:12; 13:15.

After studying these scriptures, we must look at terms. Remember, you were in school and the teacher told you that you could best understand the lesson if you studied the vocabulary words, or the high lighted words in the chapter. You are still in school, however, the instructor has changed. Yes, there is still studying, learning, memorizing, and home work. In order to graduate from God's school, you must learn how to pray, praise, and study so that you can be a productive saint. These terms will prove to be helpful as you attend church, study your Bible and just communicate with other saints.

DEFINITIONS

Amen— English and Greek, both transliterations of Hebrew, from root meaning confirm or support. "So let it be," truly, indeed.

Anoint—Four kinds of anointing, to pour or rub oil or ointment.

> Ordinary (after bathing)—Luke 7:46
>
> Burial—Mark 14:8
>
> For Shields, (sacred)– 1 King 19:16
>
> For sick and wounded—Isaiah 1:6

Anointed—fruit of the Spirit must be operative for gifts of the Spirit to work freely and with power, authority, designation of God.

Bless—to adorn Him, worship Him and Praise Him.

Glory—display of His divine attributes and perfections physical manifestation of the presence of God. Culminates in the changing of the bodies of the Saints to the likeness of the glorified Lord. Phil. 3:20

Hallelujah—highest praise; It's done; an urge to praise God.

Alleluia—word used by the writers of various psalms to invite all to join them in praising God. Rev. 19:1

Laying on of Hands—Bestowal of Blessings and Benediction—Matt. 19:13, the reception of the Holy Spirit in baptism. Acts 8:17

Exalt—to lift up, to raise in status

Thanks—an expression of gratitude, appreciation for favors received.

Magnify—to enlarge, to increase in the depth of praise by the (out of the belly) praise.

Extol— to praise highly, Laud.

Rejoice— to be glad or happy, delight.

Soul—Spirit, non material ego of a man in its ordinary relationships with earthly and physical things, the immortal part of a man.

───────PART 2───────

THE SPIRIT IN ACTION

Many people read a book and enjoy it but never digest what has been read to deposit nuggets of gold into their spiritual reservoir for enhancement. The Book of Acts was chosen because it will bring forth the most exciting venture of our lives—beginning now. The information that you house in your spiritual reservoir must be acted upon. You must be able to see the Holy Ghost in action, feel the Holy Ghost power, and demonstrate that power within your life.

We will now go to a study that will change your lives, add depth and substance to your very being, enhance the spiritual intake within your very soul and release the power of the Holy Ghost within. The Book of Acts was chosen as an instrumental study to show the certainty of the instructions that was left by Christ and carried out by those Holy Ghost filled warriors for the Gospel's sake. We will obtain greater insight into the knowledge of the extension of the Church from Jerusalem to Rome via Samaria, Antioch, Asia, and Europe. The key characters will be Peter and Paul which will bring the Gospel to life. This Gospel which began with a promise to restore the kingdom of Israel will conclude with God's grace extended to the Gentiles.

As you walk through the pages of Acts, you will develop that confidence and assurance of the Holy Ghost within you. You will develop a creative atmosphere to bring forth an explosion within you to be about God's will in your life and to fulfill the divine purpose that God has designed for you.

CHAPTER 1

- The book of Acts began by the _____ _____ and first Christian in the first century.

- The real beginning was in the book of _____ Chapter and verse _____.

- We see Jesus born, washed, died under the old _____but His _____brought the New _____ through His blood.

- The _____came _____ days after Christ's death to empower the Christians to witness.

- When we read Acts, we will see a book about _____people who become filled with the _____and do great works.

- The authorship of this book is accredited to _____, the _____.

- After reading and learning Acts 1:8, we see that we must be on one _____ and _____ means no _____ of thought and heart.

CHAPTER 2

- In order to receive the fulfillment, what two things were evident?_____and _____.

- Define Proselyte.

- What is meant by "Out of"?

- What is meant by "Whosoever shall"?

- Elaborate on " God raised Jesus" (read Col. 1:27)

- In Acts 2:37, the crowd asked the question, "What shall we do? Why did they ask that questions?

- What was the reply to the question in 2:37?

- How does one receive the Baptism?

- How will signs and wonders be wrought?

- How will the church grow? (v. 47)

CHAPTER 3

- What characteristics are exemplified of Peter?

- What is gained from 3:7? Elaborate

- The statement " Can't take God's glory," has been alluded to many times, but what does it mean?

- We must be _____in the Spirit (not pretense or hypocritical), but truth _____from the _____.

List the 7 steps

-

-

-

-

-
-
-
- In 3:23, we are given a choice to be fruitful and live or to be cursed and die. Explain.

CHAPTER 4

- Entertain the thought in passage of 4:18. Can you withstand the threats?

- Looking at 4:20, what have you seen or heard? Share your experience.

- How does our relational ministry tie in with this verse?

- How can 4:23 be an example for us?

- List the four steps in 4:29.

  Must be_____

  Must be_____

  Must have a_____

  Pray for_____

- According to 4:31, what four things does prayer bring?

- List the six steps to perform a miracle.

- Who is Gamiel?

- What was his reply to the council?

- Who is Theudas?

- According to 4:33, when one receives the Holy Ghost, what does one receive?

- According to 4:34, How should we respond after a test?

CHAPTER 5

- The Holy Ghost is _____, Adds to the_____, Brings_____ (Reverence).

- Explain 5:12 and how it relates to the pastor, the altar call?

- Explain Solomon's Porch.

- Is 5:15 symbolic of idolatry? Do we follow the same procedure in our church? Explain

- How can 5:17 be applied to our lives today?

— ACTIVITY —

- Seven Steps to the Kingdom

Steps in Apprehension of a: Demon possessed person

An Intoxicated person

A prostitute

A drug addict

- How do you witness to each of the above?

- Who is the Holy Ghost?

— Background of the Holy Ghost (Holy Spirit) —-

- Give the Scripture for the Gifts of the Spirit

- List and Define each of the gifts of the Spirit

- What is listed in 1 Corinthians 12:28-31? (define each)

CHAPTER 6

- What two characteristics are exemplified in Acts 6:1?

- In 6:3, what is the position of a Deacon?

- In 6:4, What is the job of a pastor and leader?

- Name the 7 Deacons?

- In 6:6, what does the laying on of hands symbolize?

- How will miracles be wrought?

- Who were the Libertines?

Cyrenians

Alexandrians

— Story and Comment —

Stephen, a man full of faith, of the Holy Ghost and power did great wonders and miracles among the people, spoke with wisdom and the Spirit.

CHAPTER 7

- In Acts 7:35, what Godly principle is shown here?

- In Acts 7:40, the Spirit keeps you_____.

Ten extra points—

   Who is Remphan? Moloch?

- In Acts 7:51, what does the Holy Ghost cause one to do and how?

- According to Acts 7:55, what three measures does the Holy Ghost fulfill in us?

CHAPTER 8

- According to 8:1, why did the persecution take place?

- In 8:4, what happened to the Word?

- 8:1: Define consenting.

- 8:5: What was Phillip's mission?

- 8:7: What was the result of his preaching?

- 8:8: What was brought about in that city?

- 8:9: Who was Simon? Who came on the scene? What happened?

- Explain the statement "people curse around me and don't have any respect for me" Key: verse 13

- In verse 14, what does the Holy Ghost give?

- According to verse 17, why is laying on hands recorded so many times?

- What particular characteristic do you see in Acts 8:18?

- In 8:20-23, what does the Holy Ghost cause, and what is given?

- Describe the man to whom Phillip was to minister.

- What is a Eunuch? What two desires did he have?

- Who was Candace?

- What was Phillips mission, results, and reward?

CHAPTER 9

- Explain Paul's conversion.

- Why was it important for Saul as a chosen vessel unto God?

- According to 9:19, why did Saul stay with the disciples?

- Explain 9:22.

- What Biblical truth is learned from 9:23?

- What help did God give Saul?

- Differentiate between an apostle and disciple.

- Who were the Grecians?

- How did Paul's conversion affect the Churches?

- What was Peter's task, and the result?

- In verse 32, define "immediately."

When miracles are wrought at the church, it will cause the area to_____ and _____ to the Lord.

- Differentiate between healing and miracles.

- Define Palsy.

- Who was Tabitha —(Dorcas)?

- What happened to Tabitha?

- Describe the outcome of Tabitha.

CHAPTER 10

- In chapter 10, why is the story about Cornelius and Peter so important?

- Describe Cornelius.

- Why did the angel appear to Cornelius?

- What was Cornelius' tasks?

- In 10:26, what character is presented by Peter's actions?

- According to 10:28,34, in order for miracles to be wrought, what must we do?

- List the criteria for favor with God.

- Define relational ministry.

- Discuss the relational aspect in Chapter 10. Give verses.

CHAPTER 11

- According to Chapter 11, when you do a work for God, what should you expect?

- In essence, what scripture can be used for our example in chapter 11:4-18.

- Define Evangelist.

- State the verse and action in Chapter 11, the workings of an evangelist.

- Where did the name Christian derive?

- Define prophet, and what are the characteristics of a prophet?

- Define Dearth.

- List and discuss the gifts of the Spirit.

- Explain the unleavened bread.

CHAPTER 12

- In chapter 12, what is the key to Peter's release from prison? What verse?

- What hinders our prayers?

- When prayers are answered, what do we need to do according to 12:8?

- According to 12:17, what is the significance of "Testify"?

- According to 12:19, what was Herod's request?

- According to Acts 12:21, what was Herod's lot and why?

CHAPTER 13

- In 13, what method was used then, that should be used now for one to be sent on a mission?

- In 13:1, what six things should leaders do?

- Who was Elymas?

- How is a demon bound and cast out?

- When mighty works are done, what will be the results?

- In 13:15, 16, what does the Holy Ghost do for you?

- Elaborate on 13:22 to the statement, "was David perfect?" If not, why did God use Him? Does God use imperfect beings?

- In 13:30, list the six points that makes this verse so important to the gentiles?

- What part does the Holy Ghost play in 13:43, 44?

- List the three responses we should have, when requested to stop talking about God, or teaching His Word.

CHAPTER 14

- In 14, what mission was accomplished by Paul and Barnabas in Iconium?

- In 14:4, why did the apostles fall?

- In 14:8-9, what was the outstanding characteristics of the impotent man?

- Define Impotent.

- What was the results of the impotent man's healing?

- How did Barnabas and Paul respond to the peoples acclamation?

- What was the turning point of Paul's ministry in verse 19?

- According to 14:22, How do we enter into the kingdom of God?

CHAPTER 15

- In 15, what controversial issue arose?

- According to 15:4, what two things does the Holy Ghost cause you to do?

- According to 15:7-8, we see that God will not be left without a _____.

- According to 15:11, 22, 25, what does the Holy Ghost

give, bring, and dissolve?

- What men had hazarded their lives for the Gospel?

- Define Harzarded.

- Acts 15:29 shows that the Holy Ghost _____ on to _____ from...

- According to 15:31, define consolation.

- What caused the prophets and apostles to have such a drive in the Holy Ghost?

- Who was Timotheus?

CHAPTER 16

- In 16:5, how was the church established and what was the results?

- What area was the disciples forbidden and by whom?

- In 16:15, elaborate on the word constrained.

- In 16:17, what made Paul upset at the woman's saying? Why was the woman's master upset?

- In 16:20, what was the charge against Paul and Silas?

- Define Magistrate.

- In 16:22, what was Paul and Silas' punishment?

- In 16:25, what was Paul and Silas' response to their punishment? What can we glean from this experience?

- Up to this point, List at least seven characteristics of the disciples, apostles, and prophets of God.

- In 16:26, what miracle took place and what was the result.

- Looking at verse 26, how do we, many times, miss our freedom and our solutions to the problems.

- What three things does 16:37 tell us as Holy Ghost—filled believers?

CHAPTER 17

- In 17:5, define Lewd, and explain who Jason was.

- What was the result of Paul's teaching?

- In Acts 17:6, when Paul couldn't be found, what action was taken?

- Why were saints more noble in Berea than those in Thessalonica?

- In 17:14, Paul went to teach at the _____ and left _____and _____ to teach.

- What stirred Paul's spirit in Athens?

- Define Epicureans and Stoicks.

- Who was Areopagus?

- What strong thing did the Philosophers accuse Paul of preaching?

- What did the Athenians do in their past time?

- What does superstitious mean as it relates to 17:22?

- Tell about Mars Hill.

- Explain Paul's message on Mars Hill addressing the "Unknown God."

- Learn 17:28.

- Explain 17:31.

- Who were Dionysius and Damaris?

CHAPTER 18

- In the 18th chapter, who was Aquila and Priscilla?

- When people reject your witness, what should your posture be?

- Who was Justus?

- How was Crispus affected by Paul's teaching?

- In 18:9, what three aspects of consolation did God render to Paul?

- When we have the Holy Ghost, what are we assured? (18:10)

- In 18:11, what did the Jews do and who did they get to assist their actions?

- In 18:12, what was Gallios' response?

- Define Lewdness.

- Who was Sosthenes and what happened in 18:17?

- In 18:18, where did Paul go and who accompanied him? Why did Paul shave his head? Explain the vow.

- What was Paul's mission from Ephesus and Phrygia?

- Who was Apollos?

- Why was it important to mention Apollos coming to Ephesus, and what was wrong with his teaching? Who assisted him and in what way? What was the effect of Apollos' teaching?

CHAPTER 19

- According to 19:1 what was Paul's mission when he returned to Ephesus?

- What was the disciples' response to Paul and what did Paul do for the disciples?

- Explain two new things the disciples did?

- Why does the spirit come to us?

- What three things do we possess with the Spirit in persuasion of the Gospel?

- Who was Tyrannus?

- Do we get in debates over the Gospel?

- In 19:10, how long did Paul teach and to whom?

- What was the outcome of Paul's teachings in 19:11?

- What was brought from Paul's body and the result?

- Who are the seven sons of Sceva?

- What is an exorcist?

- When you don't have the Spirit and you pretend, what can the results be?

- When Jesus is lifted, what happens?

- How much is 50,000 pieces of silver?

- According to 19:22, who ministered to Paul. Describe each.

- Who was Demetrius?

- According to 19:28, what uproar did Demetrius cause and how did this affect the disciples?

- Who dismissed the assembly and how?

CHAPTER 20

- In 20:4, who accompanied Paul to Asia?

- How do we grow in Spirit?

- In 20:9, who was Eutychus and what happened?

- Explain 20:12.

- In 20:17-18, why did Paul call the elders?

- According to 20:19, 24, how are we to serve?

- According to 20:35, how are we to be blessed?

CHAPTER 21

Circle the right answer.

- According to 21:4, in ministry, we must be led by: (Choose the right answer)

A. The pastor

B. Our Spouses

C. The Spirit

D. The organized church

- Why was Phillip mentioned in 21:8?

- Who was Agabus?

- In 21:13, what does this scripture say about Paul, and to us?

- After being warned by Agabus, did Paul go to Jerusalem? How was he received?

- What four things did Paul expound on in 21:25?

- In 21:26, what accusation was brought against Paul before his seven days of preaching was ended?

- What prevented Paul's death?

- What was Paul's lot?

- According to 21:40, what was the result of Paul's lot?

- Give background of Paul.

- Who is Gamaliel?

CHAPTER 22

- In 22:4-20, briefly summarize Paul's discourse.

- Through Paul's discourse, what four things may we list?

- In 22:28, explain "free born."

- What natural defense did Paul use in 22:25?

CHAPTER 23

- Explain the procedures in 23:1-8?

- What did the Sadducees and Pharisees believe?

- What is meant by "whited wall"?

- In 23:9, what was the verdict concerning Paul? What did the chief captain do and why?

- From 23:11, what can you glean that will assist you in knowing why Paul didn't fear for his life?

- Explain the statement, "God has angels encamped for our protection" in relation to 23:16.

CHAPTER 24

- In 24:5, what accusation was made against Paul?

- Tell about each of the listed:

Ananias—

Tertullus—

Felix—

Lysias—

- According to 24:10, what is exemplary of the Spirit?

- What is a centurion?

- Who was Drusilla?

CHAPTER 25

- How long was Paul bound before he was brought before Felix?

- Who was Paul's case declared to?

CHAPTER 26

- Who was Agrippa?

- Briefly summarize Paul's conversation with Agrippa in 26:1-23.

- What did Festus accuse Paul of and why?

- What are the two personality traits of the Spirit in 26:25?

- In 26:28, how did King Agrippa respond?

- Thinking in today's time, what was missing in Paul's account to witness to King Agrippa?

- In 26:31, what was the court decision?

CHAPTER 27

- Explain why Paul could not be set free.

- Who was Paul later delivered to?

- What is the ship of Adramyttium?

- What was Myra?

- 27:6 depicts another side of Paul's lot. Explain that.

- Since the centurion did not listen, what happened to Paul?

- In 27:22, what was Paul's response to this tempestuous situation? What consolation did Paul proclaim?

- In 27:23, why could Paul speak with boldness concerning their lives.

- What message is gathered from 27:31?

- List the spiritual steps we can glean from 27:34-38.

- What Revelation is encompassed in 27:44

CHAPTER 28

- In 28:1, what made the Barbarous people think Paul was a God?

- Who lodged Paul and the group?

- What miracle was wrought by Paul? Give the result.

- What happened to Paul when he arrived in Rome? What happened after three days?

- What was the result of Paul calling the Jews together?

DIAGRAMS

The God Head

We are God's Creation

    A. We are the chosen One

We are the seed of God's Divine Thought

    A. Start small & Bloom with proper care

We are nourished by:

    A. The watering of the Spirit

    B. The miracle growth of God's grace and mercy

        1.Grace- God's unmerited favor, his enabling power

        2.Mercy- God's extended Love

        3.Love- Nutured by love, our gift(s) will develope and be effective

Cultivating-School, Sunday School, Formal Study,Prayer, Fasting and consecration

Strength, stability is explosive enough to spill over into surrounding areas!

GIFTS OF THE SPIRIT

V.S.

FRUIT OF THE SPIRIT

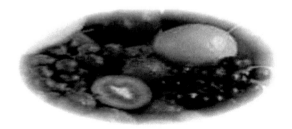

The Holy of Holies

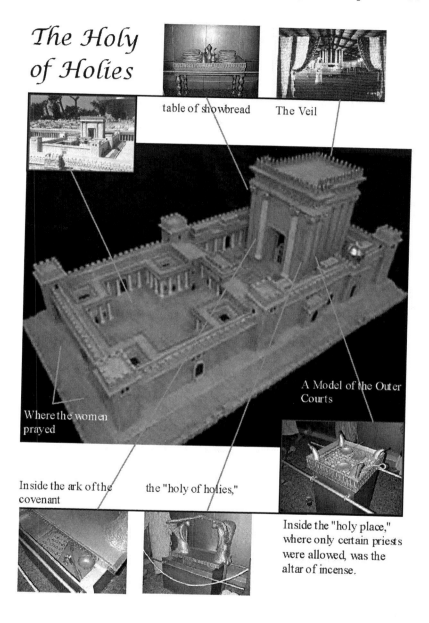

table of showbread

The Veil

A Model of the Outer Courts

Where the women prayed

Inside the ark of the covenant

the "holy of holies,"

Inside the "holy place," where only certain priests were allowed, was the altar of incense.

The Holy Ghost Explosion

Father

Son

Fruit of the Spirit

Holy Spirit

Gifts of the Spirit

Love, Goodness, Peace, Gentleness, Faith, Temperance, Joy, Meekness

Prayer & Praise

Blast Off!

PAUL'S JOURNEY

JERUSALEM to
ANTIOCH to
SELEUCIA to
CYPRUS to
SALAMIS to
PAPHOS to
SERGIUS PAULUS to
PAPHOS to
PERGA (in PAMPHYLIA) to
ANTIOCH in PISIDIA to
ICONIUM to
LYCAONIA to
LYSTRA and DERBE back to
JERUSALEM

From ANTIOCH Barnabas & Mark departed to CYRUS

From CYRUS
Paul & Silas went to
SYRIA and CILICIA
PAUL went to
DERBE to
LYSTRA to
PHRYGIA to
GALATIA to
MYSIA to
TROAS to
SAMOTHRACIA to
NEOPOLIS to
PHILIPPI (macedonia) to
AMPHIPOLIS to

APOLLONIAN to
THESSALONICA to
BEREA-(Paul & Silas sent)
ATHENS – Paul to
CORINTH to
SYRIA to
EPHESUS to
CAESAREA to
ANTIOCH to
GALATIA to
PHRYGIA to
EPHESUS to
MACEDONIA to
ACHAIA to
JERUSALEM to
MACEDONIA to
GREECE to
MACEDONIA to
ASIA to
TROAS to
ASSOS to
MITYLENE to
CHIOS to
SAMOS to
TROGYLLIUM to
MILETUS to
EPHESUS to
COOS to
RHODES to
PATAR to
PHENICIA to
CYPRUS to

SYRIA to
TYRE to
PTOLEMAIS to
CAESAREA to
ITALY to
ASAI to
SIDON to
CYPRUS to
CILICIA to
PAMPHYLLIA to
MYRA to
CNIDUS to
CRETE to
SALMONE to
LASEA to
CLAUA to
ADRIA to
MELITA to
SYRACUSE to
RHEGUIM to
PUTEOLI to
ROME

**To order more books,
Contact**

True Vine Publishing Company
P.O. Box 22448
Nashville, TN 37202

Please send_____ # of Books to:

Name: _____

Address:

_____

_____

_____

**Shipping and Handling $3.00 (1-3 books)
$ 1.25 per book beyond 3**

Total Amount Enclosed: $_____

**Or, Order online @
www.truevinepublishing.com**

HOLY GHOST EXPLOSION

PATRICIA E. DAVIS

True Vine Publishing Co.
P.O. Box 22448
Nashville, TN 37202

www.truevinepublishing.com